Introduction

Welcome to *PL/SQL in IBM DB2: A Beginner's Tutorial*. Yes, it is true; you can write, compile and run **PL/SQL** programs in IBM DB2 database. Used to be an exclusive procedural language to Oracle database, IBM DB2 now has PL/SQL.

PL/SQL

PL/SQL is the Procedural Language extension of SQL. A PL/SQL program can have *both* SQL statements and procedural statements. In the program, the SQL statements are used to access *sets* of data stored in the database, while the procedural statements are used to process *individual* data item, and to control the program flow using the if-then-else and looping structures.

About This Book

This book is for beginners. If you have no prior PL/SQL skill, and you want to learn the IBM DB2's PL/SQL the practical way, then this book is perfect for you.

However, this book does not teach you SQL. If you do not have SQL skill, please read my book, *IBM DB2 SQL for Beginners*.

This book consists of eight chapters as follows.

Chapter 1, "Setting up" is a guide to set up the DB2 environment required to try the book example.

Chapter 2, "Your First PL/SQL Programs" demonstrates how you can display Hello World in many flavors.

Chapter 3, "Blocks" is about the structure of PL/SQL programs.

Chapter 4, "Variables" shows how to declare variables and their variations.

Chapter 5, "Program Flows" covers conditional and loop statements.

Chapter 6, "Exception Handling" discusses the various techniques to handle run time errors.

Chapter 7, "SQL in PL/SQL" talks about SQL special features in PL/SQL, including cursor for processing rows returned bty SQL query.

Finally, Chapter 8, "Stored programs" shows how to write function and procedure to be stored in the database.

Coding Convention

PL/SQL is not case sensitive. In this book, however, PL/SQL reserved words such as BEGIN and EXCEPTION are printed in upper case. Other words and characters, such as variable and table names, are written in lower case.

In the book examples a single space is used between words or expressions. Extra spaces are allowed and have no effect.

Chapter 1: Setting up

To try out the examples in this book, you need a working DB2 database server and a client. Because you need to run programs, create tables and other objects, as well as store and update data, it is best if you have your own DB2 installation. Fortunately, you can download DB2 Express-C Edition for free from IBM's website.

This chapter guides you to install DB2 Express-C Edition. It also shows you how to start and stop the CLPPlus command-line client, which you use to compile, execute, and see the output of, your PL/SQL programs.

Downloading DB2 Express-C

DB2 Express-C software can be downloaded from the IBM web page,

```
http://www-01.ibm.com/software/data/db2/express-
    c/download.html
```

Select the version for your platform and follow the download instruction. You will be requested to sign in to your IBM account. If you don't have one already, create an account; it is free.

Note
The book examples are tested on Windows. They should work equally well on UNIX and the other DB2 supported platforms. The following installation guide is for Windows only.

Installing DB2 Express-C

Run your downloaded file by double-clicking it; its file name will be similar to *v10.5fp1_win_expc.exe*. You might see the Open File – Security Warning like that in Figure 1.1. If you download the file from the IBM website, don't worry, click the Run button.

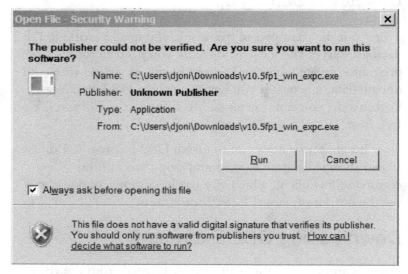

Figure 1.1: The Open File - Security Warning

The next window that will appear is your file extraction, which depends on the file extraction software you have; mine is the one in Figure 1.2. Click the Browse button and navigate to a directory of your choice. When you are done with the directory selection, and getting back to the file extraction window, click the Unzip button.

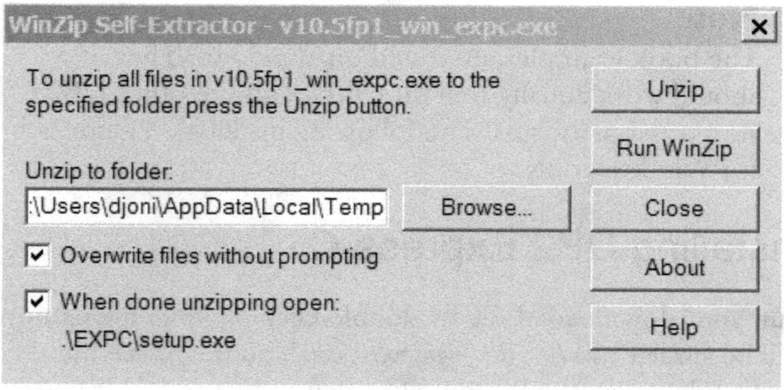

Figure 1.2: File extraction

The next window after the completion of the file extraction is the Welcome screen as shown in Figure 1.3. Select "Install a Product" from the menu listed on the left side.

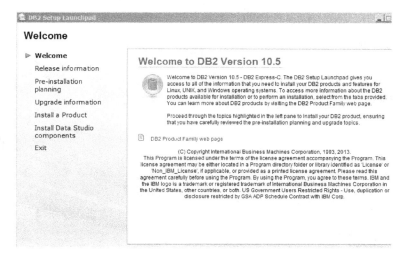

Figure 1.3: Welcoming to DB2

Your Welcome screen should now look like that shown in Figure 1.4. Click the Install New button.

6

Figure 1.4: The Summary window

When the Setup window appears (Figure 1.5) click the Next button. Then, on the License Agreement window, accept the license agreement, and click the Next button.

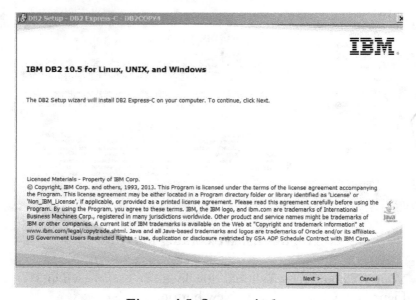

Figure 1.5: Setup window

On the Installation Type window (Figure 1.6), select Typical and click the Next button.

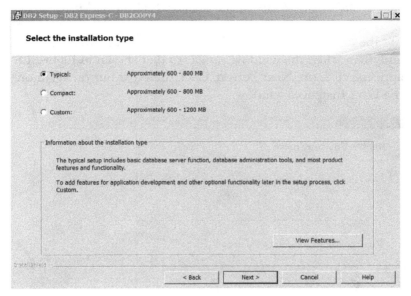

Figure 1.6: Installation Type

On the next window (Figure 1.7), select "Install DB2 Express-C on this computer" option, and click the Next button.

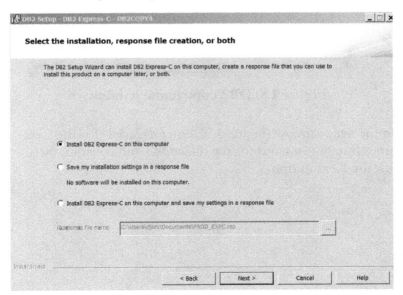

Figure 1.7: Installation/Response File window

On the next window, select the location of your installation; and, then when the window similar to that shown in Figure 1.8 appears, click the Next button. Click the Next button again on the DB2 Instances window.

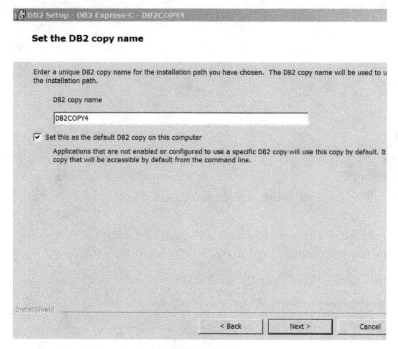

Figure 1.8: DB2 copy name window

On the next window (Figure 1.9), enter *db2admin* for the User name, enter a password for the db2admin and confirm; then, click the Next button.

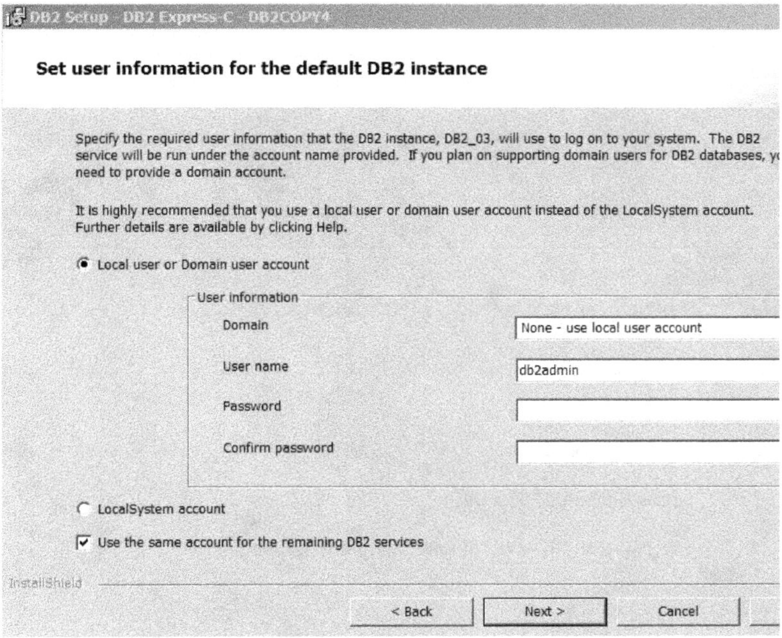

Figure 1.9: db2admin password window

On the Start copying window (Figure 1.10), click the Install button; and wait for the installation completion.

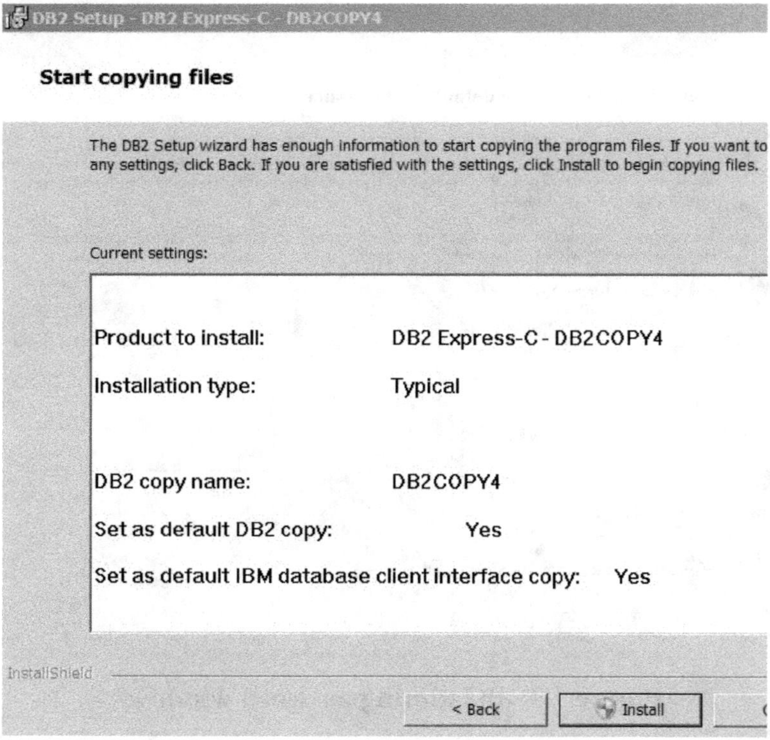

Figure 1.10: Start copying window

When the Setup completion window appears (Figure 1.11), click the Finish button, and your DB2 is ready for use.

You will next learn to use the CLPPlus command-line client.

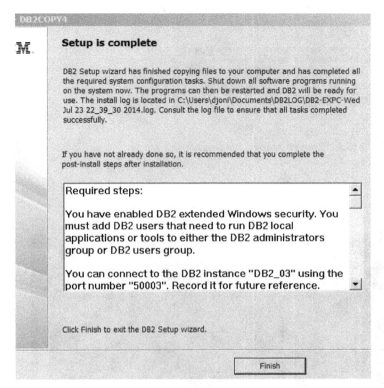

Figure 1.11: Setup completion window

Using the CLPPlus

In this book you will use CLPPlus to interact with the DB2 database server, including writing and executing PL/SQL programs. Displayable output will also be on the CLPPlus client.

Start the CLPPlus command-line client from the Windows start menu by selecting the DB2 Command Line Processor Plus.

Connect to the DB2 server using the account you use to log in to your Windows.

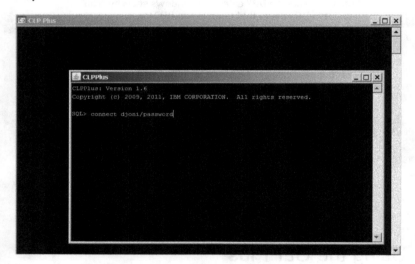

When prompted for DATABASE NAME, HOSTNAME and PORT, just press Enter key.

At the SQL> prompt, you can type in SQL statements and run them.

```
Administrator: DB2 CLP  DB2COPY1                    _ □ x
D:\DB2\BIN>db2set db2_compatibility_vector=ora

D:\DB2\BIN>db2stop
SQL1064N  DB2STOP processing was successful.

D:\DB2\BIN>db2start
SQL1063N  DB2START processing was successful.

D:\DB2\BIN>
```

Your DB2 is now set to compile and run PL/SQL programs.

Setting NULL Display

To see NULL data, rather than blank, issue a command: SET
null NULL;

Before you issue the command, when you query a table,
such as the product table, the output you see is as follows.
Notice the blanks on the PRICE and LAUNCH_DT of the
New Nut.

```
P_CODE P_NAME          PRICE LAUNCH_DT
------ --------------- ------ ----------
1      Nail            10.00 2013-03-31
2      Washer          15.00 2013-03-29
3      Nut             15.00 2013-03-29
4      Screw           25.00 2013-03-30
5      Super_Nut       30.00 2013-03-30
6      New Nut
```

After you issue the SET null NULL command, you will NULL
instead of blank.

```
P_CODE P_NAME          PRICE LAUNCH_DT
------ --------------- ------ ----------
1      Nail            10.00 2013-03-31
2      Washer          15.00 2013-03-29
3      Nut             15.00 2013-03-29
```

```
4        Screw              25.00 2013-03-30
5        Super_Nut          30.00 2013-03-30
6        New Nut             NULL NULL
```

Closing CLPPlus

To close CLPPlus, enter and execute EXIT on the SQL prompt.

You are now set to test the book examples.

Chapter 2: Your First PL/SQL Programs

The purpose of this chapter is to show you what PL/SQL programs look like and to briefly introduce some of the PL/SQL features.

Displaying a String

To display a "Hello World" string, we use the PL/SQL-supplied dbms_output.put_line procedure. Example 2.1 is a PL/SQL program that uses the procedure with Hello World string as its parameter.

Example 2-1: Hello World

```
BEGIN
  dbms_output.put_line ('Hello World');
END;
```

Note that string must be enclosed in single quotes.

To display the string in CLPPlus, you need to execute the **set serveroutput on** command as shown on the following screenshot.

```
CLPPlus                                    _ □ ×

Database Connection Information :
----------------------------------
Hostname = localhost
Database server = DB2/NT  SQL10051
SQL authorization ID = DJONI
Local database alias = SAMPLE
Port = 50000

SQL> set serveroutput on
SQL> |
```

Entering and Running PL/SQL Program

You enter a source code by typing in line-by-line on your CLPPlus screen; then run a PL/SQL program by entering a forward slash (/)

The following screenshot shows Example 2-1 entered and run. The result is the display of the Hello World string and a feedback indicating the program is successful.

```
CLPPlus                                        _ □ ×

SQL> BEGIN
   2    DBMS_OUTPUT.PUT_LINE('Hello World');
   3 END;
   4 /
Hello World

DB250000I: The command completed successfully.

SQL> |
```

Variable

Example 2-2 also displays a Hello World, but the string is not the parameter of the dbms_output.put_line procedure. The parameter in this example is now an expression of a variable named *greeting* concatenated with an exclamation mark. (The double pipes | | is the concatenation operator).

Example 2-2: String variable

```
DECLARE
  greeting VARCHAR (11);
BEGIN
  greeting := 'Hello World';
  dbms_output.put_line (greeting || '!');
END;
```

The display now looks like the following.

18

Hello World!

Numerical Manipulation

The previous two examples manipulate string data; Example 2-3 is a program that manipulates numerical data. SQRT is a built-in function; it returns the square root of its parameter.

Example 2-3: Numerical data

```
DECLARE
  multiplication DECIMAL (6, 2);
BEGIN
  DBMS_OUTPUT.PUT_LINE (2 * 10);
  multiplication := 2 * 10;
  DBMS_OUTPUT.PUT_LINE (multiplication);
  DBMS_OUTPUT.PUT_LINE (SQRT (multiplication - 4)) ;
END;
```

The output display will be:

```
20
20.00
4.0E0
```

SQL Statement

One of the PL/SQL distinct features is its tight integration with the database; for example, a PL/SQL program can have SQL statements.

To quickly gain SQL skill, read my book,

"IBM DB2 SQL for Beginners."

Example 2-4 has three SQL statements. The INSERT, UPDATE and DELETE statements, respectively adds, updates, and deletes the rows of the *product* table.

Example 2-4: SQL statements

```
BEGIN
  INSERT INTO product VALUES
    (9999, 'Test', NULL, NULL, NULL);
  UPDATE product SET price = 0 WHERE p_code = 9999;
```

```
   DELETE FROM product WHERE p_code = 9;
END;
```

Run the SQL statement in Example 2-5 to create the product table.

Example 2-5: Creating product table

```
CREATE TABLE product
   (
     p_code      INTEGER NOT NULL,
     p_name      VARCHAR(15),
     p_type      VARCHAR(6),
     price       DECIMAL(4,2),
     launch_dt DATE,
     PRIMARY KEY (p_code)
   );
```

Then, insert six rows into the table by running the SQL statement in Example 2-6.

Example 2-6: Inserting six rows

```
INSERT INTO product
    VALUES (1, 'Apple', 'Fruit', 1, '2014-5-1'),
  (2, 'Broccoli', 'Veggie', 2, '2014-5-2'),
  (3, 'Carrot', 'Veggie', 3, '2014-5-3'),
  (4, 'Mango', 'Fruit', 4, '2014-5-4'),
  (5, 'Grape', 'Fruit', 5, '2014-5-5'),
  (9, NULL, NULL, NULL, NULL);
```

The product table, before the Example 2-4 program is executed, has the following rows.

P_CODE	P_NAME	P_TYPE	PRICE	LAUNCH_DT
1	Apple	Fruit	1.00	2014-05-01
2	Broccoli	Veggie	2.00	2014-05-02
3	Carrot	Veggie	3.00	2014-05-03
4	Mango	Fruit	4.00	2014-05-04
5	Grape	Fruit	5.00	2014-05-05
9	NULL	NULL	NULL	NULL

after running the program, the rows will be as follows.

P_CODE	P_NAME	P_TYPE	PRICE	LAUNCH_DT

```
------ -------- ------ ------ ----------
1       Apple    Fruit   1.00 2014-05-01
2       Broccoli Veggie  2.00 2014-05-02
3       Carrot   Veggie  3.00 2014-05-03
4       Mango    Fruit   4.00 2014-05-04
5       Grape    Fruit   5.00 2014-05-05
9999    Test     NULL    0.00 NULL
```

Example 2-7 demonstrates a SQL statement working together with a procedural statement. The SELECT statement retrieves the Apple row from the product table. The IF-THEN statement checks the launch date to decide if a new row with a renewed product name should be created.

Example 2-7: SQL and procedural statements

```
DECLARE
  selected_product product%ROWTYPE;
BEGIN
  SELECT * INTO selected_product
      FROM product WHERE p_name = 'Apple';
  IF TO_CHAR(selected_product.launch_dt, 'YYYYMMDD') <
      '20140705' THEN
    INSERT INTO product VALUES
      (11, 'New Apple', 'Fruit', 1.5, CURRENT_DATE) ;
  END IF;
END;
```

Here are the rows after you run the program. The "New Apple" was inserted.

```
P_CODE P_NAME     P_TYPE  PRICE LAUNCH_DT
------ ---------- ------ ------ ----------
1       Apple      Fruit   1.00 2014-05-01
2       Broccoli   Veggie  2.00 2014-05-02
3       Carrot     Veggie  3.00 2014-05-03
4       Mango      Fruit   4.00 2014-05-04
5       Grape      Fruit   5.00 2014-05-05
11      New Apple  Fruit   1.50 2014-08-02
9999    Test       NULL    0.00 NULL
```

Exception handling

When you run the program in Example 2.9 again, it will fail, the program is aborted, as the p_code column is the primary key of the product table hence duplicate value is not allowed. You get an error message that looks like the following.

```
ERROR near line 7:
SQL0803N One or more values in the INSERT statement,
    UPDATE statement, or foreign key update caused
    by a DELETE statement are not valid because the
    primary key, unique constraint or unique index
    identified by "1" constrains table
    "DJONI.PRODUCT" from having duplicate values
    for the index key.
```

PL/SQL has an exception-handling feature to handle runtime errors. In Example 2-8 we add an exception handler. The DUP_VAL_ON_INDEX exception handler traps the error encountered by Example 2-7 and gets completed successfully; it does not abort at runtime.

Example 2-8: Exception handler

```
DECLARE
  selected_product product%ROWTYPE;
BEGIN
  SELECT * INTO selected_product FROM product WHERE
      p_name = 'Apple';
  IF TO_CHAR(selected_product.launch_dt, 'YYYYMMDD') <
      '20140705' THEN
    INSERT INTO product VALUES
      (11, 'New Apple', 'Fruit', 3.1, CURRENT_DATE) ;
  END IF;
EXCEPTION
  WHEN DUP_VAL_ON_INDEX THEN
  dbms_output.put_line('Product Code already exists')
      ;
END;
```

Here is the output and feedback message you will see.

```
Product Code already exists

DB250000I: The command completed successfully.
```

Comment

In closing this chapter, I would like to introduce *comment*, which is useful as inline documentation—you can put important information about a program as comments inside its source code. Comments are ignored, not compiled, they are not executable.

Comment comes in two flavors: Single and multi-line.

Any text in a source code following a double dash -- until the end of the line, is a single-line comment. When a / * mark is encountered, all texts and lines a closing * / mark is encountered, is a multi-line comment.

Example 2-9 is functionally the same as Example 2-8 but with some comments added generously.

Example 2-9: Comments

```
/*
This program demonstrates PL/SQL exception-handling
      feature, and the two types of comment line as
      inline documentation
*/
DECLARE
  selected_product product%ROWTYPE; -- Declaring a row
      type variable
BEGIN
  SELECT * INTO selected_product FROM product WHERE
      p_name = 'Apple';
-- the next lines up to END IF are procedural
      statements
  IF TO_CHAR(selected_product.launch_dt, 'YYYYMMDD') <
      '20140705' THEN
    INSERT INTO product VALUES
      (11, 'New Apple', 'Fruit', 3.1, CURRENT_DATE) ;
  END IF;
EXCEPTION  /* the exception handling starts here,
      EXCEPTION is its reserved word */
  WHEN DUP_VAL_ON_INDEX THEN
  dbms_output.put_line('Product Code already exists')
      ;
END;
```

23

Chapter 3: Block

PL/SQL is a block-structured programming language. A PL/SQL program consists of one or more blocks.

A block has three parts: Declaration, Executable and Exception-handling. A block has the following structure.

```
DECLARE
  Declaration
BEGIN
  Executable
EXCEPTION
  Exception-handling
END;
```

The three parts of a block are separated by the DECLARE, BEGIN, EXCEPTION, and END, which are PL/SQL reserved words. You should not use these three words and any other reserved word for other than their designated purposes.

The Declaration part is where all declarations such as variable declaration must be located; the Executable part has all the executable statements; while the Exception-handling part is where you write your runtime exception-handlers.

Only the Executable part is mandatory; the Declaration and Exception_handling parts are optional.

Example 2-1 in Chapter 2 reproduced here as Example 3-1, has one executable statement only.

Example 3-1: Hello World

```
BEGIN
  dbms_output.put_line ('Hello World');
END;
```

Example 2-2 reproduced here as Example 3-2, has the Declaration part with one declaration of a variable named greeting, and the Executable part with two executable statements: An assignment statement of Hello World string using the := operator to the greeting variable and a statement that calls the dbms_output.put_line procedure to display Hello World! string.

Example 3-2: String variable

```
DECLARE
  greeting VARCHAR (11);
BEGIN
  greeting := 'Hello World';
  dbms_output.put_line (greeting || '!');
END;
```

Example 2-8 reproduced here as Example 3-3, has all three parts.

Example 3-3: Exception handler

```
DECLARE
  selected_product product%ROWTYPE;
BEGIN
  SELECT * INTO selected_product FROM product WHERE
      p_name = 'Apple';
  IF TO_CHAR(selected_product.launch_dt, 'YYYYMMDD') <
      '20140705' THEN
    INSERT INTO product VALUES
      (11, 'New Apple', 'Fruit', 3.1, CURRENT_DATE) ;
    COMMIT;
  END IF;
EXCEPTION
  WHEN DUP_VAL_ON_INDEX THEN
  dbms_output.put_line('Product Code already exists')
      ;
END;
```

Block Nesting

You can write a program with multiple blocks by nesting a block under another block.

In the Executable part of Example 3-4 we have a total of four blocks with three levels of nesting. The parent block has two nested children. The second child has a child, the grandchild of the parent block.

Listing 3.4: Nesting in Exception-handling part

```
BEGIN -- parent
  dbms_output.put_line('Parent block');
  BEGIN -- first child
    dbms_output.put_line('  First child nested
      block');
  END;
  BEGIN -- second child
      dbms_output.put_line('  Second child nested
      block');
   BEGIN -- grandchild
     dbms_output.put_line('    Grandchild nested block
       under second child');
    END;
  END;
END;
```

The program's output looks like the following.

```
Parent block
  First child nested block
  Second child nested block
    Grandchild nested block under second child
```

Variable Visibility

Parent's variables are visible (can be used) in all its nested blocks. In Example 3-5, the parent_var is visible in its child's block.

Listing 3-5: Variable visibility

```
DECLARE
parent_var VARCHAR(10) := 'parent';
BEGIN
    BEGIN
      dbms_output.put_line(parent_var);
    END;
END;
```

Here is the output.

```
parent

DB250000I: The command completed successfully.
```

However, a variable declared in a nested block is neither visible to its parent block nor to other children blocks. In Example 3-6 the first_child_var is not accessible by its parent.

Listing 3-6: Child's variable not visible by parnet

```
BEGIN
  dbms_output.put_line(first_child_var);

    DECLARE -- first child
      first_child_var VARCHAR(20) := 'first child';
    BEGIN
      dbms_output.put_line(first_child_var);
    END;

END;
```

When you run the program, you will get the following error message.

```
ERROR near line 2:
SQL0206N "FIRST_CHILD_VAR" is not valid in the context
      where it is used.
```

In Example 3-7 the sibling_var is not accessible by its sibling (second child).

Listing 3-7: Sibling's variable not visible

```
BEGIN

    DECLARE -- first child
      sibling_var VARCHAR(10) := 'sibling';
    BEGIN
      dbms_output.put_line(sibling_var);
    END;

    BEGIN -- second child
      dbms_output.put_line(sibling_var);
    END;
END;
```

When you run the program, you will get the following error message.

```
ERROR near line 10:
```

```
SQL0206N "SIBLING_VAR" is not valid in the context
         where it is used.
```

Nesting in Exception-handling part

All previous nesting's are in the Executable part. You can also block nesting in the Exception-handling part as demonstrated in Example 3-8. In this example, the Exception-handling part has a block (parent) with a nested block (child); this parent block also has an exception-handler. (You will learn about error codes, such as +100 and -1422 in this example, in Chapter 6)

Listing 3.8: Nesting in Exception-handling part

```
DECLARE
   code_var        INTEGER;
   type_var        CHAR(6);
   name_var        VARCHAR (20);
   price_var       DECIMAL(4,2);
   update_dt_var DATE;
BEGIN
   SELECT p_code, p_type, p_name, price, launch_dt
   INTO code_var, type_var, name_var, price_var,
        update_dt_var
   FROM product
   WHERE p_name = 'Pineapple';
   dbms_output.put_line (code_var||' '||type_var||' '||
   name_var ||' '||price_var ||' '||update_dt_var);
EXCEPTION -- parent exception
WHEN OTHERS THEN
   BEGIN -- a parent block nested in the Exception-
         handling
      IF SQLCODE IN(-438, -803) THEN
         BEGIN -- a child block
            IF SQLCODE = -438 THEN
               dbms_output.put_line('there is no
            Pineapple');
            ELSE
               dbms_output.put_line('query returns more
            than one row');
            END IF;
         END;
      END IF;
```

```
   EXCEPTION -- Exception-handling of the nested
      parent block
      WHEN OTHERS THEN
      NULL;
  END;
END;
```

As there is no Pineapple in the product table, you will see the following output from the program.

```
there is no Pineapple

DB250000I: The command completed successfully.
```

Chapter 4: Variables

Variable is introduced in Chapter 2. You use variable to hold program data. When the program ends, the variable and its data are no longer available (To preserve (persist) the data you need to store them in the database.)

Variables must be declared before they can be used by any executable statement. Here is the syntax of variable declaration:

variable_name datatype;

A variable name must start with a letter; the rest can be letters, digits, or any of the following three symbols: _ (underscore), # (number sign), and $ (dollar sign). The maximum length of a name is 30 characters. PL/SQL is not case sensitive. Additionally, variable name must not be reserved word. You can find the complete list of reserved words in the IBM DB2 manuals.

Note that a declaration must be terminated by a semicolon.

The following six variable names, for example, are not valid for the reasons indicated.

```
9code_var -- start with numeric
9Code_Var -- case insensitive hence same reason as
      previous one
price% -- has a % character
Name var -- has a blank
Date_the_price_of_this_produce_was_changed_var --
      longer than 30 characters
BEGIN -- a reserved word
```

Example 4-1 has a non-valid 9code_var variable name. Note that the NULL executable statement does nothing.

Example 4-1: Invalid Variable Name

```
DECLARE
  9code_var VARCHAR (20);
BEGIN
NULL;
```

```
END;
```

When you run the program, you will get the following error message.

```
SQL0103N The numeric literal "9code_var" is not valid.
```

As long as they are no longer than 30 characters and enclosed in double quotes, though not recommended, you can still use such names. In the Executable and Exception parts, when you use the names, you must continue to have their double quotes, as demonstrated in Example 4-2.

Example 4-2: Variable Name with Double quotes

```
DECLARE
  "9code_var" VARCHAR (20);
BEGIN
"9code_var" := 1 + 2;
END;
```

The program is successful.

```
DB250000I: The command completed successfully.
```

If the variable is not quoted in the Executable as in Example 4-3, the program fails.

Example 4-3: Variable Name with Double quotes

```
DECLARE
  "9code_var" VARCHAR (20);
BEGIN
  9code_var := 1 + 2;
END;
```

You get the same error message as you did in Example 4-1.

```
SQL0103N The numeric literal "9code_var" is not valid.
```

Variable Declaration

Although the Declaration part is optional, as mentioned earlier, any variable used in Executable part must be declared; otherwise, the program will fail.

In Example 4-4, code_var used in the INTO clause of the SELECT statement is not declared.

Example 4-4: Non-declared Variable

```
DECLARE
  name_var       VARCHAR(20) ;
  price_var      DECIMAL(4, 2) ;
  launch_dt_var DATE;
BEGIN
  SELECT p_code
  , p_name
  , price
  , launch_dt
  INTO code_var
  , name_var
  , price_var
  , launch_dt_var
  FROM product
  WHERE p_name = 'Apple';
END;
```

When you run the program, the PL/SQL compiler complains that code_var was not declared, the program does not get executed.

```
SQL0206N "CODE_VAR" is not valid in the context where
         it is used.
```

Datatype

When you declare a variable, you must specify its datatype. We used the following first five data types in Chapter 3, Example 3-8.

- INTEGER - to store numeric integer type of data
- CHAR - to store fixed length string of characters.
- VARCHAR (m) - to store a variable length string of characters to a maximum of m characters.
- DECIMAL (p, s) - to store numeric data with precision of p digits and scale of s digits
- DATE – date
- BOOLEAN – to store TRUE or FALSE value

In Example 4-5 higher_price is a Boolean variable. In the Executable this variable is set to TRUE if the price of Carrot is higher than 2.5. Then, on the next line, if it is TRUE the message is displayed; otherwise do nothing (the NULL statement).

Example 4-5: Boolean Variable

```
DECLARE
  name_var      VARCHAR(6) ;
  code_var      VARCHAR(6);
  price_var     DECIMAL(4, 2) ;
  launch_dt_var DATE;
  higher_price BOOLEAN ;
BEGIN
  SELECT p_code
  , p_name
  , price
  , launch_dt
  INTO code_var
  , name_var
  , price_var
  , launch_dt_var
  FROM product
  WHERE p_name = 'Carrot';
    IF price_var > 2.5 THEN higher_price:=TRUE;
      IF higher_price then dbms_output.put_line('The
      price of our   Carrot is indeed higher than
      2.5');
         ELSE NULL;
       END IF;
    END IF;
END;
```

Other Data types

In addition to these five data types, PL/SQL supports other data types such as FLOAT (floating point number) and CLOB (Character Large Object Binary). Please consult the DB2 manuals available online on the Oracle website about the other data types not covered in this book.

%ROWTYPE

ROWTYPE data type anchors (refers) to the data types of all columns of a table *row*.

You have seen ROWTYPE in Chapter 2. Here is Example 2-7 reproduced as Example 4-6. The selected_product variable is anchored to the column data types of the product table.

The columns are implicitly declared within the row declaration; the selected_product.launch_dt in the IF statement is an example.

Note the use of the dot notation to refer to the individual column.

Example 4-6: SQL and procedural statements

```
DECLARE
  selected_product product%ROWTYPE;
BEGIN
  SELECT * INTO selected_product
      FROM product WHERE p_name = 'Carrot';
  IF TO_CHAR(selected_product.launch_dt, 'YYYYMMDD') <
      '20140705' THEN
    INSERT INTO product VALUES
      (21, 'New Carrot', 'Veggie', 1.5, CURRENT_DATE);
    COMMIT;
  END IF;
END;
```

%TYPE

If you need to anchor to the data type of a specific column, use the %TYPE as shown in Example 4-7 where launch_dt_var is anchored to the launch_dt column.

Example 4-7: SQL and procedural statements

```
DECLARE
  launch_dt_var product.launch_dt%TYPE;
BEGIN
  SELECT launch_dt INTO launch_dt_var
      FROM product WHERE p_name = 'Carrot';
```

```
IF TO_CHAR (launch_dt_var, 'YYYYMMDD') < '20140705'
    THEN
  INSERT INTO product VALUES
    (31, 'Next Mango', 'Fruit', 1.5, CURRENT_DATE);
  COMMIT;
 END IF;
END;
```

Initial Value

When you declare a variable you can assign its initial value using the following syntax. If you do not change the value; the initial values is the variable's *default* value.

```
variable_name data_type := 'initial_value';
```

In Example 4-8 the p_type_var is initialized to 'Fruit', which is then used as a value in the INSERT statement.

Example 4-8: SQL and procedural statements

```
DECLARE
  code_var product.p_type%TYPE := 'Fruit';
BEGIN
   INSERT INTO product VALUES
     (41, 'Grape', code_var, 7, CURRENT_DATE);
END;
```

Constant

A constant is a variable with a fixed value assigned during its declaration; you cannot change the value. The syntax of a constant declaration is as follows.

```
variable_name CONSTANT data_type := 'initial_value';
```

In Example 4-9 the type_con holds the 'Fruit' value for life.

Example 4-9: SQL and procedural statements

```
DECLARE
  type_con CONSTANT product.p_type%TYPE := 'Fruit';
BEGIN
   INSERT INTO product VALUES
     (71, 'Melon', type_con, 9, CURRENT_DATE);
```

```
END;
```

The program will fail if it tries to change the value of a constant. In Example 4-10 the program tries to change the value of type_con.

Example 4-10: SQL and procedural statements

```
DECLARE
   type_con CONSTANT product.p_type%TYPE := 'Fruit';
BEGIN
   type_con := 'Veggie';
   INSERT INTO product VALUES
      (81, 'Spinach', type_con, 9, CURRENT_DATE);
END;
```

When you run Example 4-9, you will see an error as follows.

```
SQL20547N The statement failed because the target of
      an assignment is a read-only variable. Variable
      name: "TYPE_CON".
```

Chapter 5: Program Flows

The executable statements in all preceding examples are
executed linearly from top to the bottom of the programs. In
this chapter you will learn conditional and loop statements to
control the execution flow of a program.

Conditional and Loop statements in a Block

Conditional and loop statements are executable statements.

Here is the block structure again.

```
DECLARE
   Declaration
BEGIN
   Executable
EXCEPTION
   Exception handler
END;
```

As conditional and loop statements are executable statements,
they must be located between the BEGIN and EXCEPTION
reserved words. As the Exception-handler part is optional, if a
program does not have it, then the exception and loop
statements are between the BEGIN and END reserved words.

An executable statement must be terminated by a
semicolon.

Control Statements

To control program flows, you use conditional and loop
statements.

IF

The IF control statements have three versions: IF THEN, IF
THEN ELSE, and IF THEN ELSEIF.

IF THEN

The syntax of the IF THEN statement is.

```
IF condition THEN
   statements;
END IF;
```

Only if the condition is true the statements will be executed.

You have seen an IF THEN statement in Example 2-7, reproduce here as Example 5-1. In this program, the INSERT statement will only be executed when the launch_dt of Apple is earlier than April 5, 2014.

Example 5-1: IF THEN statement

```
DECLARE
   selected_product product%ROWTYPE;
BEGIN
   SELECT * INTO selected_product
       FROM product WHERE p_name = 'Apple';
   IF TO_CHAR(selected_product.launch_dt, 'YYYYMMDD') <
       '20140705' THEN
     INSERT INTO product VALUES
       (11, 'New Apple', 'Fruit', 1.5, CURRENT_DATE) ;
   END IF;
END;
```

IF THEN ELSE

The syntax of the IF THEN ELSE statement is.

```
IF condition THEN
   if_statements;
ELSE
   else_statements;
END IF;
```

An IF THEN ELSE executes its if_statements if its condition is true. If the condition is false, the else_statements are executed.

Example 5-2 has an IF THEN ELSE statement. It is Example 5-1 with the ELSE clause added. The ELSE and its

NULL statement add clarity that the program will *not* do anything unless the launch_dt of Apple is earlier than April 5, 2014.

Example 5-2: IF THEN ELSE statement

```
DECLARE
  selected_product product%ROWTYPE;
BEGIN
  SELECT * INTO selected_product
      FROM product WHERE p_name = 'Apple';
  IF TO_CHAR(selected_product.launch_dt, 'YYYYMMDD') <
      '20140705' THEN
    INSERT INTO product VALUES
      (11, 'New Apple', 'Fruit', 1.5, CURRENT_DATE) ;
    ELSE NULL;
  END IF;
END;
```

IF THEN ELSIF

If you need multiple ELSE's, then use an IF THEN ELSIF statement. Its syntax is as follows.

```
IF condition_1 THEN
   statements_1;
ELSIF condition_2 THEN
   statements_2;
ELSIF ...
[ ELSE
   else_statements ]
END IF;
```

The IF THEN ELSIF statement executes only the first statement for which its condition is true; the remaining conditions are not evaluated. If no condition is true, then the else_statements are executed, if they exist. The ELSE is optional.

Example 5-3 has an IF THEN ELSIF statement. Depending on the launch_dt of the Apple, a New Apple with either p_code 11 or 12 will be inserted.

Example 5-3: IF THEN ELSIF statement

```
DECLARE
```

```
  selected_product product%ROWTYPE;
BEGIN
  SELECT * INTO selected_product
      FROM product WHERE p_name = 'Apple';
  IF TO_CHAR(selected_product.launch_dt, 'YYYYMMDD') <
      '20140705' THEN
    INSERT INTO product VALUES
      (11, 'New Apple', 'Fruit', 1.5, CURRENT_DATE);
   ELSIF TO_CHAR(selected_product.launch_dt,
      'YYYYMMDD') BETWEEN  '20140705' AND '20140805'
      THEN
    INSERT INTO product VALUES
      (12, 'New Apple', 'Fruit', 1.5, CURRENT_DATE);
    ELSE NULL;
  END IF;
END;
```

CASE

If you have many decision alternatives, a CASE statement might be a better a conditional statement than the IF ELSIF statement. You can choose one of the two CASE statements: Simple or Searched.

Simple CASE

The syntax of the Simple CASE statement is as follows.

```
CASE selector
WHEN selector_value_1 THEN then_statements_1;
WHEN selector_value_2 THEN then_statements_2;
WHEN ...
[ELSE else_statements]
END CASE;
```

The selector is a literal or a variable.

The simple CASE statement runs its first then_statements for which their selector_value equals the selector; the remaining WHEN statements are not executed. If no selector_value equals the selector, the CASE statement runs the else_statements.

In the Simple CASE statement of Example 5-4 the selector is the price variable. The CASE statement has three WHEN's; the output displayed depends on the price of the Apple. If the price not 1 or 2 or 3, then the displayed output is "No match".

Example 5-4: Simple CASE statement

```
DECLARE
  selected_product product%ROWTYPE;
BEGIN
  SELECT * INTO selected_product
       FROM product WHERE p_name = 'Apple';
  CASE selected_product.price
  WHEN 1 THEN
    dbms_output.put_line('Price is $1');
  WHEN 2 THEN
    dbms_output.put_line('Price is $2');
  WHEN 3 THEN
    dbms_output.put_line('Expensive');
  ELSE dbms_output.put_line('No match');
  END CASE;
END;
```

CASE_NOT_FOUND Exception

If there is no match and ELSE is not available you will get an error message as demonstrated by Example 5-5.

Example 5-5: Simple CASE statement with error

```
DECLARE
  selected_product product%ROWTYPE;
BEGIN
  SELECT * INTO selected_product
       FROM product WHERE p_name = 'Apple';
  CASE selected_product.price
  WHEN 1 THEN
    dbms_output.put_line('Price is $1');
  WHEN 2 THEN
    dbms_output.put_line('Price is $2');
  WHEN 3 THEN
    dbms_output.put_line('Expensive');
  END CASE;
END;
```

When you run the program you will see:

```
SQL0773N The case was not found for the CASE
         statement.
```

You can add a supplied CASE_NOT_FOUND exception handler to mitigate the problem as shown in Example 5-5.

Example 5-6: Simple CASE statement with exception handling

```
DECLARE
  selected_product product%ROWTYPE;
BEGIN
  SELECT * INTO selected_product
      FROM product WHERE p_name = 'Apple';
  CASE selected_product.price
  WHEN 1 THEN
    dbms_output.put_line('Price is $1');
  WHEN 2 THEN
    dbms_output.put_line('Price is $2');
  WHEN 3 THEN
    dbms_output.put_line('Expensive');
  END CASE;
EXCEPTION
  WHEN CASE_NOT_FOUND THEN dbms_output.put_line('No
      match');
END;
```

When you run Example 5-6, the exception handler traps the error and 'No match' will dispayed.

Searched CASE

A Searched CASE statement has the following syntax. Notice that it does not have a selector.

```
CASE
WHEN condition_1 THEN statements_1
WHEN condition_2 THEN statements_2
WHEN...
ELSE else_statements
END CASE;
```

While in the Simple CASE, the "condition" of selecting which statements to execute is the comparison of the selection_value to the selector for equality, in Searched CASE the condition is within each WHEN.

The searched CASE statement executes the first statement for which its condition is true. Remaining conditions are not evaluated. If no condition is true, the CASE statement runs else_statements if they exist and raises the predefined exception CASE_NOT_FOUND otherwise.

The conditions are independent; they do not need to have any kind of relationship.

Two or more conditions can be true, but only the first in the order you have in the source program (top to bottom) will be granted and its statements executed.

Example 5-7 has a Searched CASE with two conditions.

Example 5-7: Searched CASE statement

```
DECLARE
  max_price DECIMAL(6,2);
  avg_price DECIMAL(6,2);
BEGIN
  SELECT MAX(price) INTO max_price FROM product;
  SELECT AVG(price) INTO avg_price FROM product;
  CASE
    -- reduce price
  WHEN max_price > 5 THEN
    UPDATE product SET price = price - (price * .01);
    -- increase price
  WHEN avg_price < 3.5 THEN
    UPDATE product SET price = price + (price * .01);
  END CASE;
END;
```

Assuming our product table has the following rows,

P_CODE	P_NAME	P_TYPE	PRICE	LAUNCH_DT
1	Apple	Fruit	1.00	2014-05-01
2	Broccoli	Veggie	2.00	2014-05-02
3	Carrot	Veggie	3.00	2014-05-03
4	Mango	Fruit	4.00	2014-05-04
5	Grape	Fruit	5.00	2014-05-05

43

when your run Example 5-7, the first condition is not satisfied, and then, the second condition is satisfied, hence the rows of the product table are now as follows.

```
P_CODE P_NAME     P_TYPE  PRICE LAUNCH_DT
------ ---------- ------ ------ ----------
1      Apple      Fruit   1.01 2014-05-01
2      Broccoli   Veggie  2.02 2014-05-02
3      Carrot     Veggie  3.03 2014-05-03
4      Mango      Fruit   4.04 2014-05-04
5      Grape      Fruit   5.05 2014-05-05
```

LOOP

Loops allow you to repeat the same statements. LOOP statement comes in three flavors: Basic, Nested, and Fixed Iteration.

Basic LOOP

The structure of the Basic LOOP is
```
<<label>> LOOP
statements
END LOOP;
```

The statements run from the first to the last before the END LOOP, and then back to the first, until an EXIT conditional statement, which should be provided within the loop, is satisfied on which the loop is terminated.

The label is optional, but it helps clarifies the scope of the loop.

The loop in Example 5-8 iterates three times. On the fourth iteration num = 4, hence the exit condition is satisfied, the next statement after the loop is executed, and then the program ends.

Example 5-8: Basic loop
```
DECLARE
  num INTEGER := 1;
```

44

```
BEGIN
  << basic_loop >>
  LOOP
    IF num > 3 THEN -- loop three times only
      EXIT;
    END IF;
    dbms_output.put_line ('In loop: num = ' ||
      TO_CHAR(num));
    num := num + 1;
  END LOOP basic_loop;
  -- On EXIT, execute the following statement
  dbms_output.put_line('After loop: num = ' ||
      TO_CHAR(num));
END;
```

When you run the program you will get the following output.

```
In loop: num = 1
In loop: num = 2
In loop: num = 3
After loop: num = 4
```

Nested LOOP

You can nest a loop. In Example 5-9 the inner loop is nested within the outer loop. For each iteration of the outer loop, the inner loop is iterated twice.

Example 5-9: Nested loop

```
DECLARE
  counter1 INTEGER := 1;
  counter2 INTEGER := 1;
BEGIN
  LOOP
    IF counter1 > 2 THEN EXIT; -- loop twice
    END IF;
    dbms_output.put_line ('Outer loop: counter1 = ' ||
      TO_CHAR(counter1));
    counter1 := counter1 + 1;
    LOOP
      IF counter2 > 2 THEN EXIT; -- loop twice
      END IF;
      dbms_output.put_line ('Inner loop: counter2 = '
      || TO_CHAR(counter2));
      counter2 := counter2 + 1;
```

45

```
   END LOOP;
   counter2 := 1;
  END LOOP;
  dbms_output.put_line('After loop: counter1 = ' ||
      TO_CHAR(counter1));
END;
```

Here is the output of the program.

```
Outer loop: counter1 = 1
Inner loop: counter2 = 1
Inner loop: counter2 = 2
Outer loop: counter1 = 2
Inner loop: counter2 = 1
Inner loop: counter2 = 2
After loop: counter1 = 3
```

Fixed Iteration

If you know exactly the number of iteration, you can use the following loop structure.

```
FOR i IN l..u
  LOOP
    statements;
  END LOOP;
```

i the loop index, l the lower bound and u is the upper bound of the index. The index value starts with l when the loop is entered, and increments by 1; the last iteration is when the index reaches u.

In Example 5-10, the dbms_output.put_line statement inside the loop is executed three times as for this example i= 1 and u = 3.

Example 5-10: Fixed iteration loop

```
BEGIN
  FOR i IN 1..3
  LOOP
    dbms_output.put_line('Iteration number: '||i);
  END LOOP;
END;
```

The output is you expected is:

```
Iteration number: 1
Iteration number: 2
Iteration number: 3
```

WHILE loop

You can also use a WHILE to form a loop. Its syntax is as follows.

```
WHILE condition LOOP
statements;
END LOOP;
```

The statements in the loop will be executed as long as the condition is true. You must ensure the loop can terminate.

Example 5-11 does the same as Example 5-10; its loop terminates when i = 4. Notice that the i variable used here must be declared; while in Example 5-11, should not be declared. When i reaches 4 the loop ends, the statements inside it are not executed.

Example 5-11: WHILE loop

```
DECLARE
  i INTEGER := 1;
BEGIN
  WHILE i < 4
  LOOP
    dbms_output.put_line('Iteration number: '||i);
    i := i +1;
  END LOOP;
END;
```

The output will be as follows.

```
Iteration number: 1
Iteration number: 2
Iteration number: 3
```

Chapter 6: Exception-handling

You have seen examples that have Exception-handling part in the previous chapter. This chapter covers exception-handling in detail.

To restate, the purpose of putting exception-handling is to prevent runtime program failure.

The syntax of an exception handling statement is:

```
WHEN exception_handler THEN exception_statements;
```

All exception-handling statements must be located between the EXCEPTION and END reserved words.

Though optional most if not real-life PL/SQL programs have exception-handling.

Predefined Exception-handler

Here is Example 2-8 reproduce here as Example 6-1. **DUP_VAL_ON_INDEX** is one the predefined exception-handlers. This handler traps unique key violation error which happens when the program tries to add a row with an existing key value (p_code column into the product table).

Example 6-1: DUP_VAL_ON_INDEX predefined exception-handler

```
DECLARE
  selected_product product%ROWTYPE;
BEGIN
  SELECT * INTO selected_product FROM product WHERE
      p_name = 'Apple';
  IF TO_CHAR(selected_product.launch_dt, 'YYYYMMDD') <
      '20140705' THEN
    INSERT INTO product VALUES
      (11, 'New Apple', 'Fruit', 3.1, CURRENT_DATE) ;
  END IF;
EXCEPTION
  WHEN DUP_VAL_ON_INDEX THEN
```

```
      dbms_output.put_line('Product Code already exists')
         ;
END;
```

OTHERS is another predefined exception-handler. Example 3-8, reproduced here as Example 6-2, uses this handler twice.

Example 6-2: OTHERS predefined exception-handler

```
DECLARE
   code_var        INTEGER;
   type_var        CHAR(6);
   name_var        VARCHAR (20);
   price_var       DECIMAL(4,2);
   update_dt_var   DATE;
BEGIN
   SELECT p_code, p_type, p_name, price, launch_dt
   INTO code_var, type_var, name_var, price_var,
        update_dt_var
   FROM product
   WHERE p_name = 'Pineapple';
   dbms_output.put_line (code_var||' '||type_var||' '||
   name_var ||' '||price_var ||' '||update_dt_var);
EXCEPTION -- parent exception
WHEN OTHERS THEN
   BEGIN -- a parent block nested in the Exception-
         handling
     IF SQLCODE IN(-438, -803) THEN
       BEGIN -- a child block
         IF SQLCODE = -438 THEN
           dbms_output.put_line('there is no
       Pineapple');
         ELSE
           dbms_output.put_line('query returns more
       than one row');
         END IF;
       END;
     END IF;
     EXCEPTION -- Exception-handling of the nested
        parent block
       WHEN OTHERS THEN
       NULL;
   END;
END;
```

49

NO_DATA_FOUND is another commonly used exception-handler. You use it to handle error caused by a query that does not return any row, as demonstrated in Example 6-3.

Example 6-3: NO_DATA_FOUND predefined exception-handler

```
DECLARE
  pineapple product%ROWTYPE;
BEGIN
  SELECT * INTO pineapple FROM product
  WHERE p_name = 'Pineapple';
EXCEPTION
WHEN NO_DATA_FOUND THEN
  dbms_output.put_line('Our query does not find any
      Pineapple.');
END;
```

Note: Please consult the IBM DB2 manuals to look up the complete list of predefined exceptions and their usage.

Combining Exceptions

If you want the same exception action for different exception-handlers, you can put them into one exception. The syntax is then as follows.

```
WHEN exception1 OR exception2 OR . . .
THEN exception_action
```

Example 6-4 has one exception with two predefined handlers. While the DATA_NOT_FOUND handles when the SELECT INTO query returns no row, the OTHERS handles any other error than the DATA_NOT_FOUND.

Example 6-4: Combining exceptions

```
DECLARE
  code_v VARCHAR(20);
BEGIN
  SELECT p_code INTO code_v FROM product
WHERE p_name = 'Pineapple';
EXCEPTION
```

```
WHEN NO_DATA_FOUND OR OTHERS THEN
  dbms_output.put_line ('Error with the query');
END;
```

As there is no Pineapple in the product table, when you run the program, the NO_DATA_FOUND exception-handler handles the runtime error and displays the message:

```
Error with the query
```

Visibility of Exception

Similar to the scope of a variable, an exception handler in a nested block is visible only within itself.

In Example 6.5 the parent's SELECT query does not return any row. It does not have any NO_DATA_FOUND exception handler. As the first_child's no_data_found exception is not visible to the parent, the program will fail.

Example 6-5: No NO_DATA_FOUND visible to the parent

```
DECLARE
  code_v VARCHAR(20);
BEGIN
  SELECT p_code INTO code_v FROM product WHERE p_name
      = 'Guava';
    BEGIN
    SELECT p_code INTO code_v FROM product WHERE
      p_name = 'Apple';
    EXCEPTION
      WHEN no_data_found THEN
      dbms_output.put_line ('Child's Exception');
    END;
  EXCEPTION
WHEN TOO_MANY_ROWS THEN
  dbms_output.put_line ('Parent Exception');
END;
```

You will see the following outputs.

```
ERROR near line 5:
SQL0438N Application raised error or warning with
    diagnostic text:
```

"NO_DATA_FOUND".

On the other hand a parent's exception handlers can handle its children's exceptions if the children do not have the applicable handlers.

In Example 6.6, the child's SELECT statement does not return any row, as it does not have DATA_NOT_FOUND exception-handler, its parent's NO_DATA_FOUND exception-handler takes control.

Example 6-6: Parent's NO_DATA_FOUND handles its child exception

```
DECLARE
  code_v VARCHAR(20);
BEGIN
  BEGIN
    SELECT p_code INTO code_v FROM product WHERE
      p_name = 'Pineapple';
  EXCEPTION
  WHEN TOO_MANY_ROWS THEN
    dbms_output.put_line ('Child Exception');

  END;
EXCEPTION
WHEN NO_DATA_FOUND THEN
  dbms_output.put_line ('Parent Exception');
END;
```

Here is the output.

Parent Exception

DB250000I: The command completed successfully.

SQLCODE and SQLERRM functions

PL/SQL provides SQLCODE and SQLERRM functions; when you call these functions, they will return the Oracle error code and message respectively for the error encountered by your program at run time.

Example 6-7 demonstrates the use of the two functions to display the error code and text.

Example 6-7: SQLCODE and SQLERRM functions

```
DECLARE
  code_v VARCHAR(20);
BEGIN
  BEGIN
    SELECT p_code INTO code_v FROM product WHERE
      p_name = 'Pineapple';
  EXCEPTION
  WHEN TOO_MANY_ROWS THEN
    dbms_output.put_line ('Child Exception');
  END;
EXCEPTION
WHEN OTHERS THEN
  dbms_output.put_line (SQLCODE || ': '|| SQLERRM);
END;
```

You will see the error code and text on the output as Pineapple is not available in the product table; and, it turns out the exception-handler is the NO_DATA_FOUND and its error code is -438.

```
-438: SQL0438N  Application raised error or warning
      with diagnostic text:
 "NO_DATA_FOUND".  SQLSTATE=ORANF

DB250000I: The command completed successfully.
```

Defining DB2 Error

You might have an error that does not have a pre-defined exception. Fortunately, PL/SQL has a feature to solve it known as PRAGMA EXCEPTION_INIT. You first declare an EXCEPTION in the Declaration part using the following syntax.

```
exception_name EXCEPTION;
```

where exception_name is the name of your choice.

Then, also in the Declaration part, you define that exception with the following syntax.

```
PRAGMA EXCEPTION_INIT(exception_name, error_code);
```

where exception_name is the name of the exception you already declare. Here is a partial list of the error code from the DB2 manual. The error code we need is in the first column (PLSQLCODE).

PLSQLCODE	PLSQLNAME	DB2CODE	DB2STATE
-1	DUP_VAL_ON_INDEX	-803	23505
+100	NO_DATA_FOUND	+100	02000
-1012	NOT_LOGGED_ON	-1024	08003
-1017	LOGIN_DENIED	-30082	08001
-1476	ZERO_DIVIDE	-801	22012
-1722	INVALID_NUMBER	-420	22018
-1001	INVALID_CURSOR	-501	24501
-1422	TOO_MANY_ROWS	-811	21000
-6502	VALUE_ERROR	-433	22001
-6511	CURSOR_ALREADY_OPEN	-502	24502
-6532	SUBSCRIPT_OUTSIDE_LIMIT	-20439	428H1
-6533	SUBSCRIPT_BEYOND_COUNT	-20439	2202E
-6592	CASE_NOT_FOUND	-773	20000

In Example 6-8 the UPDATE tries to update a primary key to an existing value, causing a unique constraint error. As seen on the above list, the error number for violating unique constraint violation is -1.

Example 6-8: Defining DB2 error

```
DECLARE
pk_violation EXCEPTION;
PRAGMA EXCEPTION_INIT(pk_violation, -1);
BEGIN
  UPDATE product SET p_code = 1 WHERE p_code = 2;
EXCEPTION
WHEN pk_violation THEN
  dbms_output.put_line (SQLCODE);
 dbms_output.put_line (SQLERRM);
END;
```

When you run Example 6-8, you will see the following output.

```
-803
```

```
SQL0803N  One or more values in the INSERT statement,
    UPDATE statement, or foreign key update caused
    by a DELETE statement are not valid because the
    primary key, unique constraint or unique index
    identified by "1" constrains table
    "DJONI.PRODUCT" from having duplicate values
    for the index key. SQLSTATE=23505
```

Note that the -803 on the output is the third column on the above list (DB2CODE)

User Defined Exception

All previous exceptions were run-time errors. You can also define your own exceptions that are not run-time errors, and let the Exception part handle these user-defined exceptions in the same fashion as run-time error exceptions.

In Example 6-9, we want any price higher than 4.5 as an exception, hence we declare it. We then use it within the IF THEN statement as the target of a RAISE statement (RAISE is a reserved word). The Exception part must have a handler for the exception as in the Exception handling part of the program.

```
DECLARE
    code_var        INTEGER;
    type_var        CHAR(6);
    name_var        VARCHAR (20);
    price_var       DECIMAL(4,2);
    launch_dt_var   DATE;
    price_too_high EXCEPTION;
BEGIN
    SELECT p_code, p_type, p_name, price, launch_dt
    INTO code_var, type_var, name_var, price_var,
        launch_dt_var
    FROM product
    WHERE p_name    = 'Grape';
    IF price_var > 4.5 THEN
```

```
    RAISE price_too_high;
  END IF;
EXCEPTION
WHEN price_too_high THEN
  dbms_output.put_line ('Price is too high');
END;
```

As the price of Grape is 5.5, the price_too_high exception is raised and you see the following out from the exception-handling part of the problem.

```
Price is too high
```

Chapter 7: SQL in PL/SQL

You have seen in the previous examples that PL/SQL programs can have both *procedural statements* and *SQL statements*. In this chapter we will focus on the SQL special features as used in PL/SQL.

First of all, let's review the three SQL statements used to maintain data: INSERT, UPDATE and DELETE. Here is Example 2-4 reproduced as Example 7-1. As you can see in this example, the three SQL statements are just the regular SQL statements you use outside of PL/SQL.

Example 7-1: SQL statements

```
BEGIN
  INSERT INTO product VALUES
    (9999, 'Test', NULL, NULL, NULL);
  UPDATE product SET price = 0 WHERE p_code = 9999;
  DELETE FROM product WHERE p_code = 9;
END;
```

When you run the PL/SQL program all statements are sent together to the database server. All results will also be sent back once to the client, such as all output displays by the dbms_output.put_line back to the CLPPlus. The 'bundling' of the SQL statements in a PL/SQL program hence, in addition to the other advantages of a compiled language, potentially reduces the client-server traffic.

INTO clause

A SELECT statement in PL/SQL has an INTO clause applicable only within PL/SQL programs.

The SELECT with INTO syntax is:

```
SELECT select_columns INTO into_columns FROM ...
```

The into_columns must be in the sequence and the same datatype as those of the select_columns. Example 7-2 has a SELECT statement that has three INTO columns.

Example 7-2: INTO clause

```
DECLARE
  code_v  VARCHAR(20);
  name_v  VARCHAR(20);
  price_v DECIMAL(6,2);
BEGIN
  SELECT p_code, p_name, price
  INTO code_v, name_v, price_v
  FROM product
  WHERE p_name = 'Apple';
  dbms_output.put_line('The price of our ' || name_v
      ||
  ' (its code is '||(code_v)|| ') is $' || price_v);
END;
```

The output of Example 7-2 looks like the following.

```
The price of our Apple (its code is 1) is $1.10

DB250000I: The command completed successfully.
```

One Row Only

A SELECT INTO must return exactly one row.

Example 7-3 fails as its query returns more than one row.

Example 7-3: More than One Row returned

```
DECLARE
  code_v  VARCHAR(20);
  name_v  VARCHAR(20);
  price_v DECIMAL(6,2);
BEGIN
  SELECT p_code, p_name, price
  INTO code_v, name_v, price_v
  FROM product;
  dbms_output.put_line(
  'The price of our ' ||name_v||
  ' (its code is '||(code_v)|| ') is $'
  || price_v);
END;
```

```
ERROR near line 6:
```

```
SQL0811N  The result of a scalar fullselect, SELECT
      INTO statement, or VALUES INTO statement is
      more than one row.
```

You can use the PL/SQL predefined TOO_MANY_ROWS exception to handle this error.

Example 7-4: Multiple Rows causing runtime error

```
DECLARE
  code_v  VARCHAR(20);
  name_v  VARCHAR(20);
  price_v DECIMAL(6,2);
BEGIN
  SELECT p_code, p_name, price
  INTO code_v, name_v, price_v
  FROM product
  WHERE p_type = 'Veggie';
EXCEPTION
WHEN TOO_MANY_ROWS THEN
dbms_output.put_line('More than one row returned');
END;
```

When you run Example 7-4, the exception-handler will displays the exception text:

```
More than one row returned
```

SELECT for UPDATE

When you need to first SELECT and then UPDATE the selected row, and you want to be sure the selected row is not updated by any other SQL statement while you are updating it, you can lock the selected row using the FOR UPDATE clause as shown in Example 7-5.

Example 7-5: Locking with FOR UPDATE clause

```
DECLARE
  p_row produce%ROWTYPE;
  price_count INTEGER := 0;
BEGIN
  SELECT * INTO p_row FROM produce
```

```
  WHERE name = 'Apple' FOR UPDATE OF price;
  UPDATE produce SET price  = 1 WHERE name = 'Apple';
END;
```

When you run the program, the Apple's price will be updated to 1 even when the row is being accessed by any other user or application.

Cursor

If you need to access more than one row, use a cursor. A cursor stores the rows return by the cursor's query; the cursor then facilitates you access the rows **one by one**.

You specify the query that you use to get the rows from a database by declaring a cursor. The declaration syntax is:

```
DECLARE
CURSOR cursor_name IS query;
```

In Example 7-6 we declare a cursor named c, which stores all products returned by its query.

Example 7-6: Cursor Declaration

```
DECLARE
  CURSOR c
  IS
    SELECT * FROM product;
... Other declarations
BEGIN
  ...
END;
```

Cursor Life Cycle

Once you declare a cursor, in the executable part, you go through the cursor's life cycle, i.e. open the cursor; fetch a row, when you are done with the cursor, close it.

The syntax of the OPEN, FETCH, and CLOSE statements are respectively:

```
OPEN cursor;
```

```
FETCH cursor INTO variable;

CLOSE cursor;
```

The FETCH has an INTO clause, which stores the row of the cursor into the variables. All data types of the variables must match with the data types of the columns of the cursor's row.

In Example 7-7, to match the data types of the cursor's columns, c_var variable is declared as a ROWTYPE of the cursor.

The program has only one FETCH, which fetches the first row from the cursor, stores it into the c_var. The p_code and p_name columns of that c_var row are then displayed. Note the use of the dot notation to select the columns.

Example 7-7: Cursor life cycle

```
DECLARE
  CURSOR c
  IS
    SELECT * FROM product;
  c_var c%ROWTYPE; -- c_var is declared as the
      cursor's rowtype
BEGIN
  OPEN c;
  FETCH c INTO c_var;
  dbms_output.put_line(c_var.p_code || ' ' ||
      c_var.p_name);
END;
```

The output display of the program is as follows.

```
1 Apple

DB250000I: The command completed successfully.
```

To access more than one row from a cursor, use loop. Example 7-8 is a program that uses a loop to process all rows in the cursor. The loop must have an exit. An easy way to exit a loop is to apply an EXIT WHEN %NOTFOUND as seen in this example.

Example 7-8: Looping through a cursor

```
DECLARE
  CURSOR c
  IS
    SELECT * FROM product;
  c_var c%ROWTYPE; -- c_var is declared as the
      cursor's rowtype
BEGIN
  OPEN c;
  LOOP
    EXIT WHEN c%NOTFOUND;
        FETCH c INTO c_var;
        dbms_output.put_line(c_var.p_code || ' ' ||
      c_var.p_name);
  END LOOP;
END;
```

When you successfully run the program, all code and name in the product table will be displayed.

```
1 Apple
2 Broccoli
3 Carrot
4 Mango
5 Grape
```

Cursor Attributes

The %NOTFOUND in Example 7-9 is one of the cursor attributes; the others are %ISOPEN, %FOUND, and %ROWCOUNT.

The use of the %ISOPEN is demonstrated in Example 7-4. The c cursor queries the name column from the produce table and stores it into name_var variable. The IF %ISOPEN statement checks the status of the cursor and if it finds the cursor is still open, it will be closed.

Note that the dbms_output.put_line can only display string. As %ISOPEN attribute is a Boolean data type while the dbms_output.put_line procedure can only display a string, we use the s variable to store the string message that we want to display.

62

Example 7-9: Applying the %ISOPEN cursor attribute

```
DECLARE
  CURSOR c
  IS SELECT p_name FROM product;
  name_c VARCHAR(5);
  s      VARCHAR(25);
BEGIN
  OPEN c;
   LOOP FETCH c INTO name_c;
    EXIT WHEN c%NOTFOUND;
    IF c%ISOPEN THEN s := 'c is still Open';
       dbms_output.put_line(s);
    END IF;
   END LOOP;
  CLOSE c;
    IF NOT c%ISOPEN THEN s := 'c is already Closed';
       dbms_output.put_line(s);
    END IF;

END;
```

Here is the output:

```
c is still Open
c is still Open
c is still Open
c is still Open
c is still Open
c is already Closed

DB250000I: The command completed successfully.
```

PL/SQL Variable in the Query

A cursor's query can include PL/SQL variable.

The cursor's query in Example 7-10 uses price_increase variable in its second output column. This column is added to the produce's unit_price; the sum is aliased as new_price.

Example 7-10: Variable in the cursor's query

```
DECLARE
  price_increase DECIMAL(2,2) := 0.01;
  CURSOR c
```

63

```
  IS
    SELECT price, (price + price_increase) new_price
    FROM product;
  C_var c%rowtype;
BEGIN
  OPEN c;
    FETCH c INTO c_var;
    dbms_output.put_line('The current price of ' ||
      c_var.price ||
  ' will increase to ' || c_var.new_price);
  CLOSE c;
END;
```

The string will be displayed on the output.

```
The current price of 1.10 will increase to 1.11
```

Cursor Last Row

Fetching beyond the last row does not produce any error, the value in the INTO variable is still that from last row fetched.

Example 7.11 will be completed successfully. The loop iterates six times. As the product table has five rows only and code 1 is the last code fetched, the 5th and the 6th outputs are 1.

Example 7-11: Last Row

```
DECLARE
  CURSOR c
  IS
    SELECT * FROM product;
  c_var c%rowtype;
  i INTEGER := 1;
BEGIN
  OPEN c;
  WHILE i < 7
  LOOP
    FETCH c INTO c_var;
    dbms_output.put_line(c_var.p_code);
    i := i + 1;
  END LOOP;
  CLOSE c;
```

```
END;
```

The output displays 5 twice.

```
1
2
3
4
5
5
```

```
DB250000I: The command completed successfully.
```

Cursor FOR Loop

The cursor FOR loop specifies a sequence of statements to be repeated once for each row returned by a cursor.

Example 7-12 uses a cursor FOR loop. Notice that there is no need to OPEN, FETCH and CLOSE the cursor. As there is no FETCH, you do not even need to declare any variable. Instead, the c_index implicitly fetches row by row from the c cursor.

Example 7-12: Cursor for LOOP

```
DECLARE
  CURSOR c
  IS
    SELECT p_code, p_name
    FROM product
    WHERE p_code > 2;
BEGIN
  FOR c_index IN c
  LOOP
    dbms_output.put_line(c_index.p_code ||' '||
      c_index.p_name);
  END LOOP;
END;
```

You will see the output like this.

```
3 Carrot
4 Mango
5 Grape
```

```
DB250000I: The command completed successfully.
```

Cursor FOR LOOP short cut

A statement with the following syntax effectively loops through the rows returned by the query.

```
FOR returned_rows IN
(query)
LOOP
  statements;
END LOOP;
```

No cursor is declared. You don't need to declare the returned_rows which stores the query's returned rows; the loop iterates through all of them.

In Example 7-13 all rows from the product table are returned. These rows are all processed one by one sequentially. Each of the output string, the produce's type and name, to be displayed is constructed on line 7.

Example 7-13: For Loop shortcut

```
DECLARE
  output VARCHAR(40);
BEGIN
  FOR p_row IN
  (SELECT * FROM product)
  LOOP
    Output := 'The name of this ' || p_row.p_type || '
      is: ' || p_row.p_name;
    dbms_output.put_line(output);
  END LOOP;
END;
```

All products will be displayed.

```
The name of this Fruit is: Apple
The name of this Veggie is: Broccoli
The name of this Veggie is: Carrot
The name of this Fruit is: Mango
The name of this Fruit is: Grape
```

```
DB250000I: The command completed successfully.
```

View

So far, the queries of our cursors are on tables. The query of a cursor can also be on a view.

Assume we have a view, produce_v, created using the CREATE VIEW statement as follows.

```
CREATE VIEW product_v AS
   SELECT * FROM product
   WHERE price > 2;
```

In Example 7-14, the cursor's a query is on the produce_v view you have just created. Its output will be the same as that of Example 7-7.

Example 7-14: Using a View

```
DECLARE
  CURSOR c
  IS
    SELECT p_code, p_name
    FROM product_v;
BEGIN
  FOR c_index IN c
  LOOP
    dbms_output.put_line(c_index.p_code ||' '||
      c_index.p_name);
  END LOOP;
END;
```

Commit and Rollback

A COMMIT statement commits new, deleted and updates rows persistently in the database. You can issue a ROLLBACK statement to back out changes that have not been committed.

Example 7-15 has both the COMMIT and ROLLBACK statements. The update to the Apple's price is committed if it is the only product with 1.5 price (which is the case); otherwise, the update is roll-backed.

Example 7-15: COMMIT and ROLLBACK

```
ECLARE
  p_row product%ROWTYPE;
  price_count INTEGER := 0;
BEGIN
  SELECT * INTO p_row FROM product
  WHERE p_name = 'Apple' FOR UPDATE OF price;
  UPDATE product SET price  = 1.5 WHERE p_name =
      'Apple';
  SELECT COUNT(*) INTO price_count FROM product
  WHERE price    = 1.5;
  IF price_count > 1 THEN
    ROLLBACK;
  ELSE
    COMMIT;
  END IF;
END;
```

Chapter 8: Stored programs

So far all our example PL/SQL programs are not stored in the database. This chapter introduces PL/SQL programs that you create and store in the database.

Stored program can be a stored function or a stored procedure.

Stored Function

A stored function is a user-defined function that is stored in the database. You can create a stored function using PL/SQL.

The syntax of the statement to create a function is:

```
CREATE FUNCTION function_name(parameters
    RETURN data_type)
  IS
    declarations
  BEGIN
    ...;
    RETURN returned_value;
    ...;
  EXCEPTION
    ...;
  END;
```

When you run Example 8-1, the statement creates a stored function named f_calc_new_price. f_calc_new_price takes two parameters, the existing price and the percentage of change. The function returned value has a DECIMAL data type, which is the calculated new price.

Example 8-1: Creating stored function calc_new_price

```
CREATE FUNCTION f_calc_new_price(
    exist_price DECIMAL(4,2),
    change_percentage DECIMAL(2,0))
  RETURN DECIMAL (4,2)
  IS
  BEGIN
```

```
    RETURN exist_price + (exist_price *
       change_percentage/100);
  END;
```

Once created, you can use a stored function just like you would any DB2 built-in function. The PL/SQL program in Example 8-2 has an UPDATE statement that uses the f_calc_new_price function to calculate new prices (an increase of 10%) to update the prices of all products.

Example 8-2: Using the calc_new_price function

```
BEGIN
UPDATE product SET price = f_calc_new_price(price, 10)
     ;
END;
```

If the product table has the following rows

P_CODE	P_NAME	P_TYPE	PRICE	LAUNCH_DT
1	Apple	Fruit	1.0	2014-05-01
2	Broccoli	Veggie	2.0	2014-05-02
3	Carrot	Veggie	3.0	2014-05-03
4	Mango	Fruit	4.0	2014-05-04
5	Grape	Fruit	5.0	2014-05-05

when you run the program successfully, the rows of the product table will be as follows.

P_CODE	P_NAME	P_TYPE	PRICE	LAUNCH_DT
1	Apple	Fruit	1.10	2014-05-01
2	Broccoli	Veggie	2.20	2014-05-02
3	Carrot	Veggie	3.30	2014-05-03
4	Mango	Fruit	4.40	2014-05-04
5	Grape	Fruit	5.50	2014-05-05

Stored Procedure

While a stored function returns a value, a stored procedure performs some actions.

The syntax of the statement to create a function is:

```
CREATE PROCEDURE procedure_name(parameters)
  IS declarations
  BEGIN
    ...;
    RETURN returned_value;
    ...;
  EXCEPTION
    ...;
  END;
```

Example 8-3 is an example statement for creating a stored procedure named p_calc_new_price. The procedure calculates a new price based on the values of its two parameters.

Example 8-3: Creating stored procedure

```
CREATE PROCEDURE p_calc_new_price(
    p_code_par product.p_code%type,
    change_percentage DECIMAL)
IS
  p_row product%ROWTYPE;
BEGIN
  SELECT * INTO p_row FROM product WHERE p_code =
      p_code_par;
  UPDATE product
  SET price    = p_row.price + (p_row.price *
      change_percentage/100)
  WHERE p_code = p_code_par;
END;
```

Now you can use (call) the procedure. Example 8-4 is an example PL/SQL program. p_calc_new_price is called to update the price of the product with p_code = 1.

Example 8-4: Calling stored procedure

```
BEGIN
  p_calc_new_price(1, 10) ;
END;
```

After running Example 8-4, the price of Apple will be increased by 10%.

```
P_CODE P_NAME     P_TYPE  PRICE LAUNCH_DT
------ ---------- ------ ------ ----------
```

```
1       Apple     Fruit    1.21 2014-05-01
2       Broccoli  Veggie   2.20 2014-05-02
3       Carrot    Veggie   3.30 2014-05-03
4       Mango     Fruit    4.40 2014-05-04
5       Grape     Fruit    5.50 2014-05-05
```

Notice the difference on the use of function and procedure (Example 8-2 versus Example 8-4), the function returns a value that must be assigned to a variable (price); while, the procedure performs the price update directly.

Removing Function or Procedure

You can remove a function or a procedure by executing the DROP FUNCTION function_name or DROP PROCEDURE procedure_name.

Package

You can package a collection of especially related stored programs. A package has two parts: specification and body.

The syntax of the statement to create a package specification is as follows.

```
CREATE PACKAGE package_name IS
    function_names
    procedure_names
  END;
```

The function and procedure names include the parameters and for function include the RETURN data type.

A package can have many functions and procedures.

In Example 8-5 we create a package specification named *mypack* for the function and procedure from Example 8-1 and 8-3. mypack package then has only one function and only one procedure.

Example 8-5: Creating package specification

```
CREATE PACKAGE mypack IS
```

```
-- function specification
  FUNCTION f_calc_new_price(
      exist_price DECIMAL(4,2),
      change_percentage DECIMAL(2,0))
    RETURN DECIMAL (4,2);
-- procedure specification
  PROCEDURE p_calc_new_price(
    p_code_par product.p_code%type,
    change_percentage DECIMAL);
  END;
```

The syntax of the statement to create a package body is as follows.

```
CREATE PACKAGE BODY package_name IS
    FUNCTION function_specification
    PROCEDURE procedure_specification
  END;
```

The package name must be the same as the name in the package specification. Example 8-6 is the statement to create the package body of *mypack* package.

Example 8-6: Creating package body

```
CREATE PACKAGE BODY mypack IS
-- function body
FUNCTION f_calc_new_price(
      exist_price DECIMAL(4,2),
      change_percentage DECIMAL(2,0))
    RETURN DECIMAL (4,2)
  IS
  BEGIN
    RETURN exist_price + (exist_price *
      change_percentage/100);
  END;
-- procedure body
PROCEDURE p_calc_new_price(
    p_code_par product.p_code%type,
    change_percentage DECIMAL)
IS
  p_row product%ROWTYPE;
BEGIN
  SELECT * INTO p_row FROM product WHERE p_code =
      p_code_par;
  UPDATE product
```

73

```
   SET price      = p_row.price + (p_row.price *
        change_percentage/100)
   WHERE p_code = p_code_par;
END;
END;
```

Calling Packaged Stored Program

You refer to the procedure or function in a package using the dot notation:

```
package.procedure_name(parameters)
```

```
package.function_name(parameters)
```

Assuming our product table has the following rows,

```
P_CODE P_NAME     P_TYPE   PRICE LAUNCH_DT
------ ---------- ------   ------ ----------
1      Apple      Fruit     1.00 2014-05-01
2      Broccoli   Veggie    2.00 2014-05-02
3      Carrot     Veggie    3.00 2014-05-03
4      Mango      Fruit     4.00 2014-05-04
5      Grape      Fruit     5.00 2014-05-05
```

when you execute the query in Example 8-7, which calls the f_calc_new_price function in the mypack package,

Example 8-7: Calling packaged function

```
SELECT p_name, mypack.f_calc_new_price(price, 10)
        new_price FROM product ;
```

you will get the following output.

```
P_NAME     NEW_PRICE
---------- ----------
Apple           1.10
Broccoli        2.20
Carrot          3.30
Mango           4.40
Grape           5.50
```

Removing Package

To remove a package from the database, use the DROP PACKAGE statement. To remove the mypack package, for example, run the following statement.

```
DROP PACKAGE mypack;
```

When the statement is successfully executed, the mypack package will no longer be in the database.

www.ingramcontent.com/pod-product-compliance
Lightning Source LLC
Chambersburg PA
CBHW061031050326
40689CB00012B/2759